Country House Pastimes

OLIVER GARNETT

The National Trust

When the Rain set in

A Rainy Morning
in the Country:
*a sketch by Olivia de Ros
of life at Hatfield House,
Hertfordshire, in the 1820s.*

She went to plain-work, and to purling brooks,
Old-fashion'd halls, dull aunts, and croaking rooks;
She went from op'ra, park, assembly, play,
To morning walks, and pray'rs three times a day
To pass her time 'twixt reading and bohea [black tea],
To muse, and spill her solitary tea,
Or o'er cold coffee trifle with the spoon,
Count the slow clock, and dine exact at noon;
Divert her eyes with pictures in the fire,
Hum half a tune, tell stories to the squire.

Alexander Pope's 'Epistle to Miss Blount' contrasts the urban excitements of George I's Coronation in 1714 with the sheer dullness of country life at Mapledurham, the Oxfordshire home of his friend, Teresa Blount. How did the leisured classes actually spend that extensive leisure, when the weather or the winter evenings kept them inside their country houses? And how did their servants amuse themselves in the little free time they were allowed? This book sets out to answer those questions.

There were certainly many, like Matthew Bramble in Smollett's novel *Humphry Clinker* (1771), who did not find country life dull: 'At Brambleton-hall, I have elbow-room within doors, and breathe a clear, elastic, salutary air ... I go to bed betimes, and rise with the sun – I make shift to pass the hours without weariness or regret, and am not destitute of amusements within doors, when the weather will not permit me to go abroad – I read, and chat, and play at billiards, cards or back-gammon.'

Long galleries, like that built at Hardwick Hall in Derbyshire in the 1590s, began life as places to take gentle exercise in bad weather. As you strolled along, you could enjoy the views out over the garden, or could look at the family portraits which came to be hung here – the origins of the art 'gallery'. Sometimes, the activities were more strenuous: badminton shuttlecocks were found under the floorboards of the Long Gallery at Chastleton in Oxfordshire, and the Stone Gallery at The Vyne in Hampshire somehow survived the children's games of football and cricket in the 1840s.

A Rainy morning in the Country.

Music at Knole

A viola da gamba and a lute decorate the chimneypiece in Thomas Sackville's Great Chamber (now the Ballroom) at Knole.

The Leicester Gallery (*illustrated on p. 48*) is one of four long galleries at Knole in Kent. It takes its name from Elizabeth I's music-loving favourite, Robert Dudley, Earl of Leicester, who owned the house briefly in the 1560s. In 1575 he organised the Revels at Kenilworth Castle in Warwickshire to entertain the Queen on one of her royal progresses. They included elaborate masques, dancing, songs and feats of agility by an Italian gymnast 'in goings, turnings, tumblings, castings, hops, jumps, leaps, skips, springs, gambands, somersaults, capretting, and flights, forward, backward, sideways, downward, upwards, and with sundry winding, gyrings and circumflections'. The Kenilworth Revels are said to have inspired the play scene in Shakespeare's *A Midsummer Night's Dream*, which takes place in the Great Chamber of the Duke of Athens. It was here, in the principal first-floor room of the Elizabethan country house, rather than in the Long Gallery or Hall, that such entertainments would have been staged.

When the Queen visited Knole in July 1573, she probably brought her own court musicians with her – mainly trumpeters, but also players of the sackbut, flute, lute, viol and drums. Thomas Sackville, who took possession of Knole in 1603, was also a music lover. In his youth he wrote a tragedy, *Gorboduc*, which was accompanied by music. He had his own band of musicians, who would have performed in the Chapel during services, in the minstrels' gallery above the screen in the Great Hall during major feasts, and after meals in his richly decorated Great Chamber. They included Bonaventure Ashby, who was to play at the Prince of Wales's funeral in 1612, John Miners, who was paid for 'strings bought for your lordship's Violls and Violins', and William Simmes, who wrote chamber music and anthems. In his will Sackville remembered the musicians he had employed, 'some for the voice and some for the instrument, who I have found to be honest in their behaviour and skilful in their profession, and who had often given me after the labour and painful travels of the day much recreation and contatation [contentment] with their delightful harmony'.

Frederick, Prince of Wales's Concerts at Kew and Cliveden

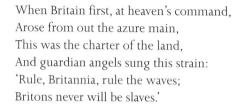

William Hogarth designed this admission ticket for the first performance of Thomas Arne's masque Alfred at Cliveden in 1740. The house and the terraced garden appear in the background.

When Britain first, at heaven's command,
Arose from out the azure main,
This was the charter of the land,
And guardian angels sung this strain:
'Rule, Britannia, rule the waves;
Britons never will be slaves.'

Even those who could afford to employ professional musicians were expected to be able to perform themselves. Elizabeth I played the virginals and possibly the lute. In 1733 George II's son, Frederick, Prince of Wales, began learning to play the bass-viol, and by the following summer was often to be seen 'with his violincello between his legs, singing French and Italian songs to his own playing for an hour or so together'. He was painted around this time rather improbably playing open-air trios at Kew with two of his sisters (*illustrated on the front cover*). What were they playing? It's unclear, but it was almost certainly *not* Handel, whom Frederick had taken against, largely it seems because the composer was supported by his much-despised father.

In 1737 the Prince took on another country house further up the Thames – Cliveden in Buckinghamshire, where music continued to be an important part of the entertainment. In 1740 he sponsored the first performance of Thomas Arne's opera, *Alfred*, to celebrate the third birthday of his daughter, Augusta. As it was August, it seemed safe to perform outside 'upon a Theatre in the Garden, compos'd of vegetables, and decorated with Festoons of Flowers', as one newspaper reported.

Frederick was so pleased with the première, which included the first performance of *Rule, Britannia*, that he demanded another the next day, 'with the Addition of some favourite Pantomime Scenes from Mr Rich's Entertainment'. But this being Britain, the weather of course intervened, and 'the Rain falling very heavy, oblig'd them to break off before it was half over; upon which his Royal Highness commanded them to finish the Masque of *Alfred* in the House'.

Country Dancing

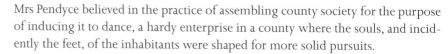

The Country Dance, an engraving by William Hogarth, 1753, that embraces the whole dancing hierarchy. In the ballroom of a Palladian country house, the elegant couple on the left dance a minuet, while the rest, who are in distinctly more rustic dress, enjoy country dancing.

Mrs Pendyce believed in the practice of assembling county society for the purpose of inducing it to dance, a hardy enterprise in a county where the souls, and incidently the feet, of the inhabitants were shaped for more solid pursuits.

John Galsworthy, *The Country House* (1907)

Galsworthy's novel, which is set in 1891, looked back somewhat sceptically on a practice that had been popular among country gentry for at least two centuries. It was much easier, in the early eighteenth century, to socialise and learn the latest dance step in town. Yet travelling long distances on bad roads in worse weather to a country house ball never seems to have been a discouragement, and most country houses had somewhere to dance.

Hospitality was an essential mark of gentility: it was expected that you would entertain your neighbours and visitors to the neighbourhood — whether you liked them or not. Dances were a chance to talk local politics, pass on gossip, and, most important of all, to find a marriage partner. This was the world in which Jane Austen grew up in the 1780s. Although only a vicar's daughter, she was invited to dances at many of the grandest Hampshire houses — Hurstbourne, Hackwood and The Vyne, and her early letters are full of gossip about such county balls, which are often central to her novels.

Polite society had to know at least the rudiments of dancing, as Lord Chesterfield explained to his son in 1745: 'I desire you will particularly attend to the graceful motion of your arms; which, with the manner of putting on your hat, and giving your hand, is all that a gentleman need attend to.' Dancing had its own hierarchy, like every other aspect of eighteenth-century society. At the bottom was country dancing — fast, furious and likely to excite the passions. *The Compleat Country Dancing-Master* (1718) describes 'The New Way of Wooing', 'The Whirlegig' and 'Rub her down with Straw', among other variations. At the top was the more graceful minuet.

Frances Bankes's Ball at Kingston Lacy, Christmas 1791

'The Ballroom was really very handsome, it was always a delightful Room and I believe you saw enough of the Ceiling [painted by Cornelius Dixon] not to think I exaggerate when I say it looked beautiful, there is a noble Lustre in the middle … you may guess it is gay and striking when the first person who went into the room called out that it looked like the Palace of Alladin.'

Country house socialising traditionally reached its climax indoors around Christmas, the season of most goodwill and least daylight. On 19 December 1791 Henry and Frances Bankes held a ball to celebrate the completion of their new ballroom at Kingston Lacy in Dorset. Frances described the night's events:

Having nearly recovered the bustle of Monday I now sit down my dear Mother with an intention to give you a particular account of the Fête; in the first place the Company were desired to be here exactly by eight, and I believe they were most of them come before nine; they were first shown into the Library ….

Upon Mr Bankes's Dressing Room Fire we kept a Quantity of Water constantly boiling, so that I flatter myself there never was so large a Company better supplied with hot Tea and Negus [punch]. I likewise saved my new Carpets very much by having nothing of that sort handed about ….

We had a very good band of Music from Salisbury, and I placed the Musicians in a half circle in the right hand Corner of the large room [the Ballroom] as you got out of the Drawing Room and of course fastened the Door that leads out to the entrance…. When the Dancing began, (there were thirty six couple) it lasted till one without ceasing, when the Eating Room and North Parlour Doors were opened, and displayed a very handsome Supper. After Supper the Dancing began again with great Spirit and lasted till about seven o'clock without any intermission. It happened fortunately that we had a much greater number of young Men than young Ladies, by which means the ugliest women in the room were sure to dance every dance unless they preferred sitting still, which kept them all in high good humour.

The Servants' Ball at Lyme, New Year's Eve 1906

The last of Frances Bankes's guests finally left at 8.30 the next morning, but her servants' long day was still not over: 'I then collected my servants and desired they would not go to bed but immediately set about cleaning the House and putting it in order; and to do them justice, when the people who had slept in the House … came down to Breakfast between eleven and twelve, the House appeared to their great astonishment just exactly in the same order as if nothing had happened.'

The country house entertainments of Mrs Bankes and her class left little leisure time for their staff. Without their own transport, it was also difficult for servants to find amusement in the local town. They were often thrown back on socialising within their own community below stairs, organising parties known as 'frolics' in the eighteenth century.

In the early nineteenth century few domestic servants received any time off, apart from church on Sunday. Gradually, however, competition from more attractive employment forced country house owners to allow their staff an afternoon off a week and a fortnight's holiday each year. By the end of the century the Yorkes of Erddig in North Wales, who had a particularly close relationship with their servants, allowed maids to stay out late three evenings a week. At the luxurious Worth Park in Sussex in the 1890s, the servants' quarters contained a reading room and library with piano, a billiard room, ballroom and theatre – all for the exclusive use of the staff. Many large houses had a regular servants' ball, and Phyllis Sandeman describes that held in Edwardian times in the Entrance Hall of Lyme Park in Cheshire:

> One of the side doors would open and Truelove [the butler], with Mrs Campbell [the housekeeper] on his arm, emerge, followed in pairs by the other servants in strict order of precedence. Strangely enough, their guests came last, for each servant was allowed to invite one friend; and thus, with the heads of the outdoor staff and their wives and the members of the house party, a sufficient company was formed to fill the large room.... the Servants' Ball at Vyne [i.e. Lyme] differed from some which were held in other great houses in that they took place above stairs not below; and that everybody from the highest to the lowest was expected to attend.

Country House Music-making in the Twentieth Century

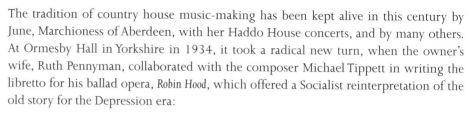

The Saloon of Hatchlands in Surrey, which now houses Alec Cobbe's famous collection of period keyboard instruments. But these are no silent museum pieces; they are regularly played at the recitals he organises each summer in the Music Room.

The tradition of country house music-making has been kept alive in this century by June, Marchioness of Aberdeen, with her Haddo House concerts, and by many others. At Ormesby Hall in Yorkshire in 1934, it took a radical new turn, when the owner's wife, Ruth Pennyman, collaborated with the composer Michael Tippett in writing the libretto for his ballad opera, *Robin Hood*, which offered a Socialist reinterpretation of the old story for the Depression era:

> So God he made us outlaws
> To beat the devil's man;
> To rob the rich, to feed the poor
> By Robin's ten-year plan.

During the Second World War, most large country houses were closed up or occupied by the forces, but even then there was still music. Joyce Grenfell remembered organising a concert by the pianist Myra Hess for the Canadian war wounded who were billeted at Cliveden:

> As we sat in the Long Drawing Room the brilliant evening light was low and the sky went pale greeny-blue after earlier rains. The view from the windows across the lawns to the woods, the river and the fields beyond was striped with long blue shadows. It didn't feel like war-time. Alice and I had arranged sofas and chairs and cushions on the floor at either end of the room; the piano was in the middle, lit by a single standard lamp, and as the daylight faded Myra was islanded in a warm pool of light; an intimate setting, and a change from the wards and public rooms the men and nurses lived in. I watched their faces as they listened to the music; for an hour or so they were in another world.

Country house music also has a more raucous side, and that tradition has been continued by the Lytton Cobbolds at Knebworth in Hertfordshire with their annual pop concerts. For many rock stars, appearing there is a highlight of their careers. As Liam Gallagher of Oasis reminded a sceptical journalist: 'God never played Knebworth.'

Dilettanti Theatricals

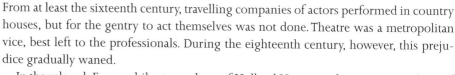

James Gillray's Dilettanti Theatricals satirises a group of stage-struck aristocrats who formed the Pic-Nic Society in 1802 to put on private theatricals, followed by a lavish supper. In the centre the bulbous Albinia, Lady Buckinghamshire of Blickling repairs her make-up and learns her part, fortified by the bottle of whisky under her dressing-table. Lady Salisbury pulls on a boot, while in the left foreground the diminutive Richard, Viscount Valletort of Cotehele in Cornwall swashbuckles as Alexander the Great.

From at least the sixteenth century, travelling companies of actors performed in country houses, but for the gentry to act themselves was not done. Theatre was a metropolitan vice, best left to the professionals. During the eighteenth century, however, this prejudice gradually waned.

In the relaxed, Francophile atmosphere of Holland House on the western outskirts of London, the Fox children often put on very sophisticated productions. In January 1761 Horace Walpole was 'excessively amused' by a performance of *Jane Shore* by the now-forgotten playwright, Nicholas Rowe ('a tragedy and therefore not worth reading', according to the fifteen-year-old Jane Austen). Among the cast were the twelve-year-old Charles James Fox, who learnt his political oratory from such performances, and his cousin, Lady Susan Fox-Strangways, who eloped with an actor three years later.

Another tragedy by Rowe, *The Fair Penitent*, was a favourite with the Delaval family, who put on an elaborate staging in the vast marble hall of their Northumberland home, Seaton Delaval, in 1790. Playing the beautiful, faithless heroine was Lord Tyrconnel's wife, Susan Delaval – 'the wildest of all her race' (and the Delavals were a notoriously wild race). A member of the audience recalled: 'Lord Delaval as Sciolto was correct and pathetic, Lady Tyrconnel mumbled her phrases but looked the thing. Lord Tyrconnel as Lothario was too bulky, his coat too scanty and he sawed the air overmuch.' More impressed was the 10th Earl of Strathmore from nearby Gibside, who was 'desperately smitten' with Lady Tyrconnel and promptly became her lover. Strathmore himself took part in the next play performed at Seaton Delaval, which could hardly have been more aptly chosen or cast: *Othello*, with Lord Tyrconnel as the Moor, Susan as Desdemona, and Strathmore as Cassio.

Jane Austen and the Dancing Marquess

Jane Austen's cousin Eliza looked forward eagerly to the Christmas of 1786 at Steventon, which promised to be 'a most brilliant party & a great deal of amusement, the House full of Company & frequent Balls'. Central to the entertainment were a series of plays in the Steventon barn, for which Jane's brother James painted scenery and wrote new epilogues. One began, somewhat pessimistically, 'Halloo, good gentlefolks! What, none asleep?' Such amateur theatricals were often more fun for the performers than the audience, as Edmund Bertram complained in Austen's *Mansfield Park* (1814), when a play is proposed: 'I would hardly walk from this room to the next to look at the raw efforts of those who have not been bred to the trade – a set of gentlemen and ladies who have all the disadvantages of education and decorum to struggle with.' The stigma of the stage remained, and, as at Seaton Delaval, the plot of the play disturbingly mirrors the human drama. When Edmund's father unexpectedly returns, rehearsals are cancelled at once.

In *Mansfield Park*, the billiard room is converted temporarily into a stage. At The Vyne, the Austens' friends and neighbours, the Chutes, built a temporary proscenium arch across one end of the Stone Gallery, where according to Caroline Chute (the model for Fanny Price in *Mansfield Park*) they at first 'only acted to a few of the house and the villagers … till our last performance … when we admitted a few of the neighbours'. Similar long galleries at Lyme and at Wimpole Hall in Cambridgeshire were used in the same way.

For the 5th Marquess of Anglesey, theatre was an obsession rather than a diversion. He had been brought up in France by the wife of the actor Constant-Benoît Coquelin – the first Cyrano de Bergerac – and he fell in love with the stage. After he inherited Plas Newydd on the Isle of Anglesey in 1898, he converted the chapel into a private theatre, where he performed in ever more exotic costume with a company of professional actors. A local newspaper reported of his performance as 'Pekoe' in *Aladdin*, 'though the lines he has to speak may not be of the highest brilliancy, [he] wears a costume that may be worth anything from £100,000 upwards'. Such extravagance inevitably led to financial ruin, and he died a bankrupt in Monte Carlo in 1905 at the age of only 30.

Cinema and Television

Lady Caroline Paget, the sister of the present Marquess of Anglesey, was painted by Rex Whistler in 1935, the year she starred in Cecil Beaton's film of The Sailor's Return.

Today, the country house provides a suitable backdrop for many a film or television costume drama. But there is also a long tradition of screening such entertainments in country houses. Before cinema, there was the magic lantern. Lord Tyrconnel's early eighteenth-century lantern still survives at Belton House in Lincolnshire. Philip Yorke II of Erddig was a particular devotee, courting his future wife, Louisa Scott, during a 'Magic Lantern Entertainment' of his slides of Scandinavia and Egypt in 1901. When film did arrive, it was welcomed by the more adventurous and American-minded country house owners like Winston Churchill, who converted the Dining Room at Chartwell into a private cinema. The particularly creative began making their own films. In the summer of 1935 at Ashcombe in Dorset, Cecil Beaton masterminded an amateur film version of David Garnett's novel, *The Sailor's Return*, with himself as the sailor, Lady Caroline Paget as the African princess, Tulip, and John Betjeman as the parson. It was a rather fraught experience. Lady Caroline's black make-up ran in the heat, and as Beaton explained, 'It is very difficult a hundred miles from London to get hold of a black baby at a moment's notice, especially on Saturday afternoons when shops are shut'. During shooting, the cast got through 300 bottles of wine, and, perhaps not surprisingly, the film was never finished.

Television brought professional entertainment into the country house on a scale not seen since the royal progresses of Elizabeth I, but a residual snobbery encouraged many owners to hide away their TV sets. The theatre designer Oliver Messel responded more imaginatively by constructing a neo-Georgian case for his sister's set, which can now be seen at Nymans in West Sussex. And at Wormsley in Buckinghamshire J. Paul Getty II has recently built a garden folly based on the Gothic Tower at Wimpole to house his satellite dish.

Learning to Draw

The Entrance Hall at Petworth, painted by Madeline Wyndham in the 1860s, when her father-in-law, the 1st Lord Leconfield (shown here), used it as a study.

During the eighteenth and nineteenth centuries, the daughters of the country gentry learned to draw, partly so that they could fill the long hours of leisure that lay ahead. In *Pride and Prejudice* (1813), the waspish Lady Catherine de Bourgh is alarmed to find that neither Elizabeth Bennet nor any of her sisters has been taught to draw: 'That is strange. But I suppose you had no opportunity. Your mother should have taken you to town every spring for the benefit of the masters.' For those unable to get to town, there were always itinerant drawing-masters like Walter Hartright, the young hero of Wilkie Collins's *Woman in White* (1859–60), who is employed to 'superintend the instruction of two young ladies in the art of painting in water-colours' at Limmeridge House in Cumberland. For this he received four guineas a week, and board and lodging, and 'was to be treated there on the footing of a gentleman'.

Most eighteenth-century amateurs painted out of doors in the great English water-colour tradition, but from about the 1820s they increasingly began to look indoors, influenced by professional genre painters like David Wilkie and then by the great mid-Victorian delineators of modern life, such as W.P. Frith and George Hicks. These amateur country house interiors are a fascinating record not only of vanished rooms, but also of vanished ways of life.

One particularly skilled amateur painter of interiors was Madeline Wyndham, whom Edith Olivier described as 'a captivating jumble of genius, beauty and charm'. She belonged to the highly artistic late Victorian world of the 'Souls', and was a friend and patron of Burne-Jones, Watts and Leighton. Not surprisingly, she became an accomplished watercolourist, and after her marriage in 1860 to Percy Wyndham, the younger son of the 1st Lord Leconfield, she often painted the interiors of his family home, Petworth in West Sussex. But she was much more than just a watercolourist. Alexander Fisher taught her to enamel on metal, which she combined with miniature painting. She was an equally skilled embroiderer, helping to found the Royal School of Art Needlework in 1872. On her travels she collected handmade lace, Italian decorated paper and much else to adorn her Wiltshire home, Clouds, the masterpiece of the Arts and Crafts architect, Philip Webb.

Painting in Oils

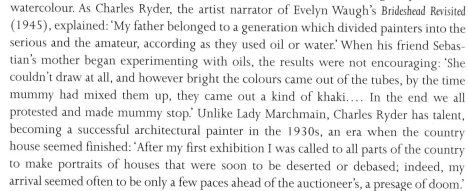

A self-portrait painted by Rebecca Dulcibella Orpen in 1885 in her painting room at Baddesley Clinton. On the easel is her unfinished oil of the house from the north-east, and in her hand she holds a mahlstick, on which she could steady her brush when working on detailed passages.

Amateurs like Walter Hartright's pupils generally stuck to sketching in pencil and watercolour. As Charles Ryder, the artist narrator of Evelyn Waugh's *Brideshead Revisited* (1945), explained: 'My father belonged to a generation which divided painters into the serious and the amateur, according as they used oil or water.' When his friend Sebastian's mother began experimenting with oils, the results were not encouraging: 'She couldn't draw at all, and however bright the colours came out of the tubes, by the time mummy had mixed them up, they came out a kind of khaki.... In the end we all protested and made mummy stop.' Unlike Lady Marchmain, Charles Ryder has talent, becoming a successful architectural painter in the 1930s, an era when the country house seemed finished: 'After my first exhibition I was called to all parts of the country to make portraits of houses that were soon to be deserted or debased; indeed, my arrival seemed often to be only a few paces ahead of the auctioneer's, a presage of doom.'

Eighty years before, skilful amateurs like Rebecca Dulcibella Orpen had painted similar country house views in watercolour and oils with less foreboding. After she was orphaned at an early age, she was taken in by her aunt, the romantic novelist and poet, Georgiana, Lady Chatterton. Lady Chatterton was also an artist, who encouraged Rebecca to learn to paint. She had a wide circle of friends and often took her niece on her country house tours in the 1850s. During these years Rebecca produced a fascinating series of watercolours recording her changing surroundings in a bright and meticulous style. In 1867 she married Marmion Edward Ferrers, the squire of Baddesley Clinton in Warwickshire. She continued to paint after her marriage, creating numerous views of Baddesley inside and out, but graduated to more sombre oils, which were better suited to evoking the dark oak furnishings of this ancient manor house.

Winston Churchill, Painter

Churchill's studio at Chartwell is hung with many of his paintings in various stages of completion.

Many remedies are suggested for the avoidance of worry and mental overstrain by persons who, over prolonged periods, have to bear exceptional responsibilities and discharge duties upon a very large scale. Some advise exercise, and others, repose. Some counsel travel, and others, retreat.

Winston Churchill, *Painting as a Pastime* (1948)

Churchill's remedy was painting, which he first took up in 1915 as a relief from the disaster of the Dardanelles campaign. Encouraged by his sister Gwendeline, he experimented with his young nephew's watercolour box, but was more attracted by oils. John and Hazel Lavery, both fine painters, and later Walter Sickert all gave him useful tuition, and he was soon taking his paints everywhere – even to the trenches of Flanders. He loved bright colour, and so particularly enjoyed painting under the Mediterranean sun of the Riviera and Morocco. He worked mainly in front of his subject, but when the weather intervened, he would retreat to the peace of his studio at the bottom of the garden at Chartwell. Churchill was modest about his talents, but characteristically fearless: 'We must not be ambitious. We cannot aspire to masterpieces. We may content ourselves with a joy ride in a paint-box. And for this Audacity is the only ticket.'

In 1948 Churchill was made an honorary Royal Academician by Sir Alfred Munnings, who shared his distaste for most modern art. Few country house owners have attempted to paint in avant-garde styles. From 1916 the painters Duncan Grant and Vanessa Bell decorated their home at Charleston in Sussex in the Bloomsbury version of French modernism, but they only rented the house, which remained part of Viscount Gage's Firle Place estate. The present Marquess of Bath, a child of the Swinging Sixties always more at home in the Chelsea Arts Club than the House of Lords, has filled the west wing of Longleat with his ambitious murals depicting Paranoia and the Ages of History. The most notorious is his Kama Sutra bedroom, whose pedigree can be traced back to works like the semi-pornographic murals by Francesco Sleter that filled the Temple of Venus at Stowe in the eighteenth century, but which have been obliterated by time or more timid successors.

Reading

A Quiet Half Hour;
by L.C. Henley, 1876,
from Hinton Ampner,
Hampshire.

'Reading is a pernicious habit. It destroys all originality of sentiment.' This was the rather surprising opinion of Thomas Hobbes, philosopher and tutor to the 2nd Earl of Devonshire in the early seventeenth century. Before the 1640s there were few books to be read in country houses. At Hardwick Hall in 1601 there were only six, which the 2nd Earl's grandmother, Bess of Hardwick, kept in her bedchamber for solemn reflection rather than relaxation. By the Restoration in 1660, some educated families had accumulated enough books to set aside a separate room for them. In the 1670s a closet was fitted up at Ham House in Surrey with bookshelves and a built-in desk for the Duke and Duchess of Lauderdale.

Although women have as a rule always been more avid readers than men, country house libraries were generally considered a male preserve until the late eighteenth century. However, in 1816 Humphry Repton noted that 'the most recent modern custom is to use the library as the general living-room', and indeed many country house watercolours from the 1820s show them being used for music, tea and other sociable gatherings of both sexes. Many Victorian novels, published as serials, were designed to be read aloud in such rooms. Florence Nightingale's father read to her every evening – something she could not abide, but which her more placid sister Parthenope accepted, as it did not interfere with her drawing.

In Trollope's novel, *The Prime Minister* (1876), Jeffrey Palliser exclaims: 'Nobody ever goes into a library to read, any more than you would go into a larder to eat', and looking at the uniformly bound sets of political pamphlets, religious tracts and agricultural treatises in many late Victorian country houses, one might ask how much they were ever actually used. But in the era before public libraries, country house collections were often intended for more than just the immediate family: the agent wanted to keep up with the latest advances in agriculture; the parson needed inspiration for next Sunday's sermon. In Samuel Richardson's novel, *Sir Charles Grandison* (1754), the idealised Grandison Hall has a library of improving literature set aside for the servants. As a child in the 1880s, H.G. Wells educated himself in the library at Uppark in West Sussex, where his mother was the housekeeper.

Letter-writing

By 1742 there can have been few country house libraries or boudoirs in Britain without a copy of Samuel Richardson's novel, *Pamela*. It was the literary sensation of the decade, a racy story of female virtue in danger, told through letters exchanged between the young heroine, Pamela Andrews, and the five other protagonists. That letters could now be sent swiftly across the whole country was thanks to the introduction of the cross-postal system twenty years before. Hitherto letters from Bath to Worcester had had to go via London; now they went direct. The instant success of the new network earned its inventor, Ralph Allen, the fortune that enabled him to build Prior Park near Bath, and made writing letters a pleasant daily routine, which reduced the isolation of country life for many.

Lady Emily Conolly, who exchanged long and frequent letters with her sisters from the 1740s until her death in 1814, wrote: 'When one receives a letter, sitting down immediately to answer it is like carrying on a conversation.' Jane Austen felt exactly the same, telling her sister Cassandra in 1801: 'I have now attained the true art of letter-writing, which we are always told, is to express on paper exactly what one would say to the same person by word of mouth; I have been talking to you almost as fast as I could the whole of this letter.'

In the age before the telephone, letters were used to pass on all the pleasures and pains of country life in an intimate, conversational style. But a certain stylistic polish was also demanded – an ability to move easily from chatty gossip to more general reflections with appropriate literary allusions. The great model was the seventeenth-century French writer Mme de Sevigné, whose affectionate letters to her daughter were published to great acclaim in England in 1725. Of course, most people's letters were never published, but they were meant to be read aloud over the breakfast table and passed on. More private details were often confided to a separate sheet, which could be extracted before circulation. For those who did not aspire to literary distinction, letter-writing was simply a way of getting through winter days in the country. As Lili Cartwright of Aynho Park in Northamptonshire wrote in her diary on 25 January 1835: 'There was nothing of note today. Sunday passed like all Sundays in writing letters in the morning and in being bored in the evening.'

Diaries

Lady Anne Clifford;
portrait attributed to
William Larkin which
can be seen at Knole.

People keep diaries for many reasons. For the Herveys of Ickworth in Suffolk, it was a family tradition. Until the end of the eighteenth century, the ostensible reason was often self-improvement, a form of confessional for the non-Catholic. Increasingly, it became more of an *aide-mémoire* – a means of recalling moments of pleasure and pain that would otherwise be lost to fading memory. It was justified as providing a record for posterity, and the travel diaries of Celia Fiennes, Lord Torrington, Horace Walpole, Mrs Lybbe Powys and many others preserve fascinating descriptions of country house life in the eighteenth century not to be found anywhere else. For women, keeping a diary was a way of establishing their own identity in an era when they were very definitely the second sex and when publishing an autobiography was socially accept-able only for men.

Lady Anne Clifford seems to have kept her Knole diary in order to document her battles to claim her vast northern inheritance. She was a formidable character, of whom it was said, 'If she will, she will, you may depend on't; if she won't, she won't, and there's an end on't.' The surviving fragment of the diary begins in 1616, when she had been married for six years to Richard, 3rd Earl of Dorset. He wanted to get his hands on Anne's money to pay for his extravagant way of life, which led to bitter arguments with her: 'He went much abroad to Cocking, to Bowling Alleys, to Plays and Horse Races, & [was] commended by all the World. I stayed in the Countrey having many times a sorrowful & heavy Heart & being condemned by most folks because I would not con-sent to the Agreement, so as I may truly say, I am like an Owl in the Desert.'

But there were happier days, such as 28 August 1616: 'In the Afternoon I wrought Stitch Work and my Lord sat and read by me'; and she recorded when they slept together. Particularly touching are the intimate details of her daughter Margaret's teething, her first steps and her childhood illnesses: 'The Child had an extreme Fit of the Ague & the Doctor sat by her all the Afternoon & gave her a Salt Powder to put in her beer' (Margaret was three at the time).

Needlework

In this panel embroidered by Mary, Queen of Scots (now at Oxburgh), a knife prunes a vine, beneath one of her favourite mottoes: *'VIRESCIT VULNERE VIRTUS'* (*'Virtue flourishes with a wound'*).

When Mary, Queen of Scots was imprisoned on the island of Lochleven in Kinross-shire in 1567, one of her first acts was to ask for her sewing things. She was sent Spanish silk, eight skeins of gold and silver thread, 4,000 pins and all the other materials she needed for her embroidery. The Scottish Queen had learnt to sew as a young woman, and over the next twenty years during the enforced leisure of her imprisonment, needlework was to be one of her few comforts.

While Mary was in the custody of Lord Shrewsbury at Tutbury Castle in 1569, a visitor 'asked her Grace since the weather did cut off all exercise abroad howe she passed the Tyme within; She sayd that all Day she wrought with her Nydill, and that the Diversitie of the Colors made the Worke seeme less tedious, and continued so long at it till veray Payn made hir to give over' (she suffered from a recurring pain in her side). Shrewsbury himself reported that she 'continueth daily resort unto my wife's chamber, where with the Lady L[ivingston] and Mrs Seaton, she sits working with the needle in which she much delights and devising of works'. Several of the embroideries which she worked alone and with Shrewsbury's wife, Bess of Hardwick, are now at Oxburgh Hall in Norfolk and at Hardwick. They show her love of *impressa* – emblems whose complex meanings are expressed through combining images, initials and wordplay.

Needlework was not just an aristocratic pastime, but an essential skill for women, in an age before sewing-machines, when most clothes were made at home, either for the family or for sale. The traditional way of teaching basic sewing skills was by producing test-pieces, known as samplers. The extensive Goodhart collection of samplers can be seen at Montacute. And when clothes wore out, they were not thrown away, but endlessly mended or recycled. 'Drizzling', or unpicking the valuable gold and silver thread from unwanted items, became a fashionable pastime in the eighteenth century; the results were kept in drizzle boxes, such as that on show in the Drawing Room at A la Ronde in Devon.

Shellwork

Jane and Mary Parminter decorated this shell alcove, which is set into the staircase leading up to the even more elaborate Shell Gallery at A la Ronde.

Shellwork was one of the most creative and elaborate of all the 'ladies' amusements' practised in eighteenth-century country houses. The oldest surviving example is probably the shell grotto at Woburn, which was built for the 4th Duke of Bedford around 1630, but shellwork became really fashionable only in the 1730s with the rise of the Rococo style, which was inspired by the shell form. In the late 1730s Sarah, Duchess of Richmond and her daughters Caroline and Emily decorated a grotto in Goodwood Park in Sussex with exotic shells brought to them in sackloads by sea captains putting in at Portsmouth. Emily and her own children in turn went on to create an even more elaborate shell cottage at Carton in Co. Kildare in 1766. Shells could also come from closer to home. In 1750 Mrs Delany, who also devoted much of her spare time to producing meticulous botanical pictures from cut paper, was decorating her bedroom at Delville: 'I am making shell-flowers in their *natural colours*, that are to go over the bow window. … The coach is at the door, and we are going to Burdoyl, a strand about six miles off, in search of shells.' Six years later, she visited Thomas Goldney's famous shell grotto in the garden of his house near Bristol and was very impressed: 'A cascade falls … over rocks, coral, shells, and is received by a bason; the walls on each hand are richly, irregularly, and very boldly adorned with everything the earth and sea can produce proper for the purpose, and all in their highest perfection.'

Overlooking the Exe Estuary in shell-rich Devon is A la Ronde, an extraordinary sixteen-sided house built in 1798 for two cousins, Jane and Mary Parminter, who had just returned from a long tour of Europe. The design is said to have been inspired by the Byzantine basilica of San Vitale in Ravenna, but instead of mosaic, they decided to decorate the upper gallery of the central octagon with shells, which were arranged in ornamental patterns and stuck to the walls with lime putty. Between the windows are panels covered with feathers, and the cousins decorated the rest of the house using a bewildering range of other materials: cork, mica, glass, broken pottery and even lichen. For the Parminters, decorating their home had been more than just a pastime.

Model-making

Betty Ratcliffe's model of the Temple of the Sun at Palmyra, which is displayed in the Gallery at Erddig.

Shells were used not only to cover walls, but also to decorate boxes like those at Arlington Court, and in making models. Perhaps the most exquisite surviving examples of the latter were made by a servant, Elizabeth Ratcliffe. She was the daughter of a Chester clockmaker and in the mid-eighteenth century went into service with the Yorkes of Erddig in North Wales. They nicknamed her 'Betty the little' to avoid confusion with an aunt of the same name. Betty inherited her father's steady hand, producing exact pencil copies of Old Master pictures and in 1767 an intricate model of William Chambers's Chinese pagoda at Kew, complete with tinkling bells.

Dorothy Yorke began to worry that Betty might be getting ideas above her station. She wrote to her son Philip in 1768: 'Pray, my dear, do not employ her in that way again for one year at least as all her improvements sink in drawing and then I shall have no service from her and make too fine a Lady of her, so much is said on that occasion that it rather puffs [her] up.' Philip, however, was keen to encourage Betty, who told him in 1770 that she would 'do the utmost of my power and endeavour to execute what you are pleas'd to request instead of comand'. The result was her most ambitious creation, a model of the ruins of the Temple of the Sun at Palmyra, made from mother of pearl and crushed mica.

The Yorkes were delighted with Betty's creeper-smothered ruins and ordered a special display case from a London craftsman, Thomas Fentham, who carved it appropriately with sun-bursts and palmettes. Dorothy also seems to have changed her mind about Betty. She educated her and came to rely on her as a companion rather than a servant. In her will she left Betty an annuity of £100, at a time when an Erddig maid earned less than £11 a year. When Dorothy died in 1787, model and case were carefully packed up and brought from her home in London to Erddig, where they have been cherished ever since.

Scrap-screens

Scrap-screens come halfway between the folio albums or more modest scrapbooks in which engravings have traditionally been kept, and the print room of the late eighteenth and early nineteenth centuries, where prints were pasted to the walls, often with decorative borders, as though they were framed paintings. They had a practical as well as a decorative function, keeping at bay the draughts which are an all too common drawback of the large country house. They also provided a conveniently portable way of dividing up long galleries and other large rooms into more intimate and welcoming spaces.

The fashion reached its height in the mid-Victorian era, when new reproductive technology was producing a mass of suitable raw material, from Christmas cards to the engravings of daily life in illustrated magazines like the *Graphic* and the *Illustrated London News*. Once the fun of snipping out and pasting down was over, such screens were often left to decay gently upstairs, as Alice Buchan, who was brought up at Elsfield Manor in Oxfordshire in the 1900s, remembers in her memoirs, which she entitled *A Scrap Screen* (1979):

> In the nurseries of my childhood there used always to be 'scrap' screens, three leaved, the leaf nearest the child's bed being almost bald because its occupant, banished to bed while it was still daylight outside, solaced its exile by picking off the scraps. Time has given them a gloss of sentiment under a yellowing varnish, through which is seen Queen Alexandra in her wedding dress, Gordon at Khartoum, the Nevsky Prospect by moonlight, snowbound travellers being dug out by St Bernard dogs with large concerned faces, and always children, with or without kittens, hoops, and spinning tops, ragged children without shoes, rich children in buttoned boots. Interspersed with these were Christmas cards of robins and windmills and tumbledown cottages. The glue dries, the scraps begin to peel, the child delightedly tears them off; no adult of my generation can see an ill-treated scrap screen without a small pang for what has been lost.

The Cholic

FISHERMAN,
of Hartlepool

Billiards

The Billiard Room at Cragside in Northumberland.

Mr Edmonstone came in when luncheon was nearly over, rejoicing that his letters were done, but then he looked disconsolately from the window and pitied the weather: 'Nothing for it but billiards. People might say it was nonsense to have a billiard-table in such a house, but for his part he found there was no getting through a wet day without them.'

Charlotte M. Yonge, *The Heir of Redclyffe* (1853)

In 1688 the Staircase Hall at Belton contained 'one billyards table with sticks and balles'. This has long since disappeared, but there is a seventeenth-century table in the Leicester Gallery at Knole (p.48) which still has its original curved cues, known as maces. Billiards, however, did not become generally popular in British country houses until the late eighteenth century, when tables were often set up in the main hall. From the early Victorian period onwards, most large houses – new and old – were given a separate billiard room, often with a smoking room attached. Because of the weight of the table's slate base, these rooms had to be on the ground floor or occasionally in the basement.

Billiard rooms are often considered to have been an exclusively male preserve, but in fact women frequently played together, or with men. In 1813 Byron declared his love for Lady Frances Webster over a game of billiards at Aston Hall in Yorkshire. He was not the only one who found it difficult to remember the score, as he confided to Lady Melbourne: 'I also observed that we went on with our game (of billiards) without counting the *hazards* – & supposed that – as mine certainly were not – the thoughts of the other party also were not exactly occupied by what was our ostensible pursuit.... P.S. 6 o'clock – This business is growing serious – & I think *Platonism* in some peril.' In *The Woman in White*, the intrepid heroine Marian Halcombe is keen for an evening game with the newly arrived Mr Hartright: 'I can match you at chess, backgammon, écarté, and (with the inevitable female drawbacks) even at billiards as well.'

Card-games

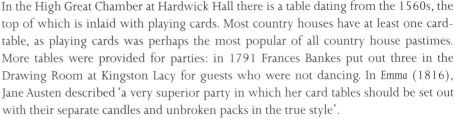

In the High Great Chamber at Hardwick Hall there is a table dating from the 1560s, the top of which is inlaid with playing cards. Most country houses have at least one card-table, as playing cards was perhaps the most popular of all country house pastimes. More tables were provided for parties: in 1791 Frances Bankes put out three in the Drawing Room at Kingston Lacy for guests who were not dancing. In *Emma* (1816), Jane Austen described 'a very superior party in which her card tables should be set out with their separate candles and unbroken packs in the true style'.

Not that Jane Austen always approved. In *Sense and Sensibility* (1811), she comments that Sir John and Lady Middleton seemed to socialise merely 'for the sake of eating, drinking, and laughing together, playing at cards, or consequences, or any other game that was sufficiently noisy'. Cards carried the added danger of gambling. Georgiana, Duchess of Devonshire gambled away huge sums at cards, but this was usually in London, at Almack's Ladies Club or Devonshire House. In the country people generally played for lower stakes. In the 1790s the immensely wealthy 3rd Duke of Dorset fretted when he lost fifteen shillings to John Hoppner, who was staying at Knole to paint his children.

Sometimes it was reputation as well as money that was at stake. In 1890, Lycett Green, the brother of the man who gave Treasurer's House in York to the National Trust, accused one of the Prince of Wales's friends of cheating at cards during a house party at Tranby Croft near Hull. The Royal Baccarat Scandal, as it became known, ended in a sensational court case, at which the Prince had to give evidence.

With typical ingenuity, the Victorians invented numerous card-games that have been more or less forgotten. 'Prof.' Louis Hoffmann's *Drawing-Room Amusements* (1879) describes Napoleon, Speculation, Spinado, Snip-Snap-Snorum, Match and Catch, Picture Pumblechook, What d'ye Buy?, The Most Laughable Thing on Earth (also known as A Trip to Paris), Ranter-go-Round, Spade the Gardener and Mixed Pickles, among many others. There were also card-games for solitary Sunday afternoons. At Chastleton in the late nineteenth century, Mary Whitmore-Jones devised many variations on Patience, and then published three guides to the subject.

Board-games

The Hardwick table is also inlaid with boards for backgammon and chess; indeed, backgammon was then known simply as 'tables'. The 9th Earl of Northumberland's Petworth accounts for 1587 record: 'PLAYE: Delivered unto your Lordshipe the some of x s. [ten shillings] to playe at tables with Mr Younge, which was loste the XXth of August.' Despite being a medium for gambling, in the eighteenth century backgammon was thought 'quite fitting for country rectors, and not derogatory to the dignity of even the higher functionaries of the Church', according to Joseph Strutt in his *Sports and Pastimes of the People of England* (1801). But Strutt also noted that the game had fallen out of fashion in recent years: 'The tables, indeed, are frequently enough to be met with in the country mansions; but upon examination you will generally find the men deficient, the dice lost, or some other cause to render them useless.' Backgammon did not really revive as a country house pastime until the 1920s.

Chess has been the king of board-games since the Middle Ages. In 1479 Sir John Paston of Caister Castle in Norfolk owned only about a dozen books, but they included *The Game and Playe of the Chesse*, which was one of Caxton's first publications. The game reached the height of aristocratic fashion thanks to the French master André Philidor, the English edition of whose *L'Analyze du jeu des Echecs* in 1777 was subscribed to by no fewer than thirteen dukes. But serious competition was then confined to London. By the mid-nineteenth century, there were good players throughout the country. George, 4th Lord Lyttelton of Hagley Hall in Worcestershire was called the 'Maecenas of English Chess' by the great American player Paul Morphy for his advocacy of the game. To a man who could translate Milton into Greek iambics while riding to hounds, chess was relatively gentle mental exercise.

The Victorian era saw a proliferation of commercially produced board-games, often with an overtly Imperialist message. Walter Jones-Whitmore of Chastleton came up with several, including *The Game of War*. Country house life as depicted in the whodunits of Agatha Christie has even inspired a board-game. *Cluedo, or Murder at Tudor Close*, was invented in 1946 by Anthony Pratt, a solicitor's clerk from Leeds, and has been popular ever since.

Further reading

CLEMINSON, Antony, 'Christmas at Kingston Lacy: Frances Bankes's Ball of 1791', *Apollo*, December 1991, pp.405–9.

CLIFFORD, D.J.H. ed., *The Diaries of Lady Anne Clifford*, Alan Sutton, 1990.

FOWLER, John, and John Cornforth, *English Decoration in the 18th Century*, Barrie & Jenkins, 1986, pp.248–53.

HORN, Pamela, *Ladies of the Manor: Wives and Daughters in Country-house Society*, Alan Sutton, 1991.

HOUFE, Simon, 'Playing with Words', *Country Life*, 31 August 1989, pp.86–8.

LUMMIS, Trevor, and Jan Marsh, *The Woman's Domain*, Viking, 1990.

MARGETSON, Stella, *Leisure and Pleasure in the 18th Century*, Cassell, 1970.

MAURIES, Patrick, *Shell Shock: Conchological Curiosities*, Thames & Hudson, 1994.

NORMAN, Clare, 'Rebecca Orpen's Country House Tour: A Portfolio of Watercolours at Baddesley Clinton', *Apollo*, April 1997, pp.28–32.

OLIVIER, Edith, *Four Victorian Ladies of Wiltshire*, Faber, 1945, pp.85–101 [Madeline Wyndham].

SACKVILLE-WEST, Vita, *Knole and the Sackvilles*, Ernest Benn, 1922.

SANDEMAN, Phyllis Elinor, *Treasure on Earth: A Country House Christmas*, Herbert Jenkins, 1952.

SOAMES, Mary, *Winston Churchill: His Life as a Painter*, Collins, 1990.

STRUTT, Joseph, *Sports and Pastimes of the People of England*, 1801.

TILLYARD, Stella, *Aristocrats*, Chatto & Windus, 1994.

WATERSON, Merlin, *The Servants' Hall*, Routledge & Kegan Paul, 1980.